MINNESOTA

Past and Present

Daniel E. Harmon

rosen publishing's
rosen
central®

New York

Published in 2010 by The Rosen Publishing Group, Inc.
29 East 21st Street, New York, NY 10010

First Edition

Library of Congress Cataloging-in-Publication Data

Harmon, Daniel E.
Minnesota: past and present / Daniel E. Harmon.—1st ed.
    p. cm.—(The United States: past and present)
Includes bibliographical references and index.
ISBN 978-1-4358-3524-5 (library binding)
ISBN 978-1-4358-8498-4 (pbk)
ISBN 978-1-4358-8499-1 (6 pack)
1. Minnesota—Juvenile literature. I. Title.
F606.3.H369 2010
977.6—dc22

2009028024

Manufactured in the United States of America

CPSIA Compliance Information: Batch #LW10YA: For Further Information contact Rosen Publishing, New York, New York at 1-800-237-9932

On the cover: Top left: A wood engraving from around 1870 shows St. Paul from Dayton's Bluff, on the east side of the Mississippi. Top right: A ship passes beneath a lift bridge at the port of Duluth. Bottom: Canoeists paddle along Duncan Lake in the Boundary Waters Canoe Area in northwest Minnesota during autumn.

Contents

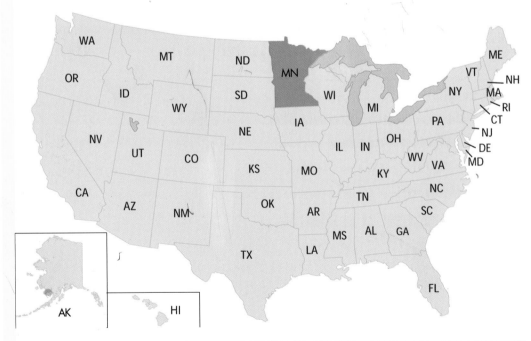

The nation's twelfth-largest state, Minnesota is located in the upper center of the country at the Canadian border. Minnesota's location has shaped its historical development.

Introduction

In 1678, French missionary Louis Hennepin and two comrades became the first Europeans to explore the headwaters of the Mississippi River. Traveling by canoe, they came upon impressive waterfalls, which Hennepin named the Falls of St. Anthony. These waterfalls would become the site of a famous American city: Minneapolis, Minnesota.

Two Native American peoples, the Dakota and Ojibwa, occupied what is now Minnesota. The land has changed dramatically. In what is today Minneapolis-St. Paul, skyscrapers stand in the place of rustic native dwellings. Industries produce electrical and machine parts, paper, and other goods used by consumers worldwide. Thousands of acres of ancient trees were cut down during the 1800s, replaced in many areas by new-growth forests, cities, and factories. Rolling plains that were once thick with buffalo herds are now farmland.

Minnesota's people have changed, too. Most Minnesotans today have European ancestry. But Native American descendants and diverse ethnic groups from Vietnam, Laos, Somalia, Ghana, and Mexico also make important contributions to the state and to the world.

Despite the changes, Minnesotans preserve their rich natural and cultural heritage. Nature lovers can thrill at the sight of moose in a silent forest and the gentle splash of a canoe paddle in a clear, remote lake. They enjoy many state and county parks. More than 150 museums depict Minnesota, past and present. Minnesota is also home to world-class orchestras and theaters.

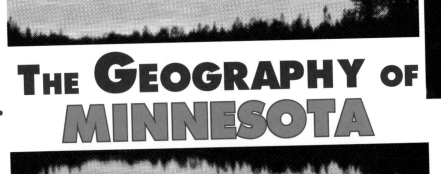

Chapter 1

THE GEOGRAPHY OF MINNESOTA

Minnesota is at the northern border of the United States, with Canada as a neighbor. To its east are the shore of Lake Superior and the state of Wisconsin. Iowa lies to the south, South Dakota to the southwest, and North Dakota to the northwest.

A careful study of the map reveals a dislocated "bit" of Minnesota that appears to enter into Canada. It is a patch of land at the northwestern corner of Lake of the Woods, a large body of freshwater that straddles the U.S.-Canada border. This isolated area, called the Northwest Angle, was the result of a surveyor error and was included as part of the United States by the oddly worded Treaty of Paris at the end of the Revolutionary War in 1783.

Minnesota is the nation's twelfth-largest state. It measures about 86,943 square miles (225,100 square kilometers) in total area. Minnesota's geographic center is about 7 miles (11 km) southwest of Brainerd, in Crow Wing County.

A Watery State

If a single word can best describe Minnesota's most prominent geographical feature, it would be "water." The state's very name means "cloudy water" in the language of the Dakota people.

Beautiful Lake Calhoun is one of many recreational lakes within view of the Minneapolis skyline. Lakes are a defining feature of Minnesota's geography.

Minnesotans proudly define their state as the "Land of 10,000 Lakes" on their license plates. Actually, the state's Department of Natural Resources reports that there are 11,842 bodies of water of at least 10 acres (4 hectares).

Red Lake in the northern part of the state is by far the largest (288,800 acres, or about 117,000 ha). Mille Lacs in east-central Minnesota is second (132,520 acres, or about 53,650 ha). Minnetonka, the third-largest lake, is within the metropolitan area of the Twin Cities: Minneapolis and St. Paul.

Lakes are not the only important waters of Minnesota. The great Mississippi River begins at Lake Itasca in the Minnesota North Woods

Minnesota's Lakes

Why does Minnesota have so many lakes? History—ancient history—gets most of the credit.

During the ice ages, glaciers covered much of what is now the United States. Some of these vast ice sheets were more than 1 mile (1.6 km) deep. They covered the land for thousands of years.

These glaciers did not lie still. They expanded and contracted, moving anywhere from 1 to 20 feet (0.3 to 6 meters) each day. In the process, the tons of moving ice altered the ground beneath them. Over time, they created high ridges and deep depressions on the earth's surface.

As the last glaciers gradually melted, they left thousands of lakes and ponds. These bodies of water became vital resources for countless life-forms, including humans. To the Dakota and Ojibwa people, they provided canoe transportation, as well as fish and other wild game for food.

Today, the lakes of Minnesota continue to delight the people who live along their shorelines, as well as visitors from nearby and far away. Most of the lakes offer boating, fishing, and swimming in rural, fir-scented surroundings. Some are in major cities. Remarkably, twenty-two natural lakes are inside the Twin Cities' municipal boundaries.

Even during the stark and frozen winter months, fishers take to the lakes. Like the region's early settlers from Scandinavia, hardy adventurers today cut fishing holes in the surface ice. Some stay on a lake for days and weeks, living in portable shelters equipped with cots, heaters, and even satellite TV and other electrical appliances powered by gas generators. They check with local authorities to learn day-to-day ice conditions and the safest places to fish. Game fish catches include walleye (the state fish), crappie, bluegill, largemouth and smallmouth bass, northern pike, trout, muskellunge (muskie), catfish, salmon, smelt, sunfish, and whitefish, among others.

and flows southward to the Gulf of Mexico. Almost 700 miles (about 1,100 km) of it are in Minnesota; the river forms part of the Minnesota-Wisconsin border. Other rivers are important for commerce and irrigation. They include the Minnesota, which crosses the southern part of the state and joins the Mississippi. The Red River of the North forms much of Minnesota's western border with North Dakota.

A ship is moored at a Duluth dock. The system of connected Great Lakes waterways allows Duluth to function as an international port for shipping.

Minnesota's "coastline" consists of approximately 120 miles (193 km) on the western shore of Lake Superior (the world's largest freshwater lake). Thanks to the opening of the St. Lawrence Seaway and a system of locks that connect all of the Great Lakes, Duluth—a Minnesota city at the western edge of Lake Superior—has become an international port. Commercial ships from Minnesota travel from Duluth through the Great Lakes system to the world beyond.

Land Features

Minnesota contains vast, rolling plains and farmland in its lower two-thirds and flatter plains in the northwest. The northeast includes

This view of Seven Sisters Prairie and Lake Christina illustrates the state's great geographical diversity. Vast prairies and farmlands enfold thousands of bodies of water.

vast wilderness and isolated lakes, and it's bordered by Lake Superior. There are a variety of land features as one travels from region to region throughout the state. Minnesota includes portions of two main geographic regions: the Superior Upland and the Central Lowland.

The Superior Upland, which lies near Lake Superior, includes rocky highlands in northeastern Minnesota. Some of this area contains rich deposits of iron, copper, and other metals. Eagle Mountain, the state's highest peak, is part of the Sawtooth Range in the Arrowhead region. Located in the Misquah Hills in the northeastern corner of the state, Eagle Mountain is within sight of Lake Superior. The shoreline of Lake Superior is Minnesota's lowest point.

The largest area of Minnesota is within the Central Lowland, part of the Interior Plains of the United States. The Central Lowland includes the Young Drift Plains of central, south-central, and western Minnesota. It also contains the so-called Driftless Area in the state's southeastern corner, an area untouched by glaciers, which borders the Mississippi River. The Dissected Till Plains (also called Prairie Hills), a flat plateau, lie in the southwest. There is a broad, flat valley in the northwest, where the Red River of the North flows. Flat plains stretch north and south of the Minnesota River and northward beyond Red Lake. In the northern part of the Central Lowland, swamps, marshes, and bogs are common features.

City and Country

The state's largest population centers grew around rivers and lakes. St. Paul is Minnesota's capital. It has a "twin" city that is more famous: Minneapolis. The Twin Cities are only 10 miles (16 km) apart along the Mississippi. They are the state's largest cities. According to 2006 U.S. Census Bureau estimates, about 373,000 people lived in Minneapolis; 273,000 in St. Paul. Roughly half the people of Minnesota live in or around the Twin Cities.

Other large Minnesota cities include Duluth and Rochester. Duluth, a city stretching along the Lake Superior coast, is the state's principal Great Lakes shipping port. Its population is approximately eighty-five thousand. Rochester, in the southeastern farming region, has about ninety-seven thousand citizens.

Away from the cities and towns, Minnesota is a state with mammoth prairie farms and beautiful woodlands. Tree species include pine, fir, birch, elm, maple, and aspen. Wildflowers and shrubs abound throughout the state.

Animal life is plentiful, too. Minnesota has more timber wolves and bald eagles than any other state except Alaska. Its 78 mammal species include beavers, black bears, coyotes, flying squirrels, foxes, gophers, moose, muskrats, opossums, salamanders, and snakes. It has 29 reptile species, 22 amphibian species, and more than 400 bird species.

Red-breasted mergansers take to the Brooks River just after sunrise. Mergansers are among the more than 400 bird species that live in Minnesota.

Minnesota is an excellent locale for birding, especially for naturalists interested in waterfowl. Common loons are definitely "common" in Minnesota: An estimated twelve thousand live there. (The common loon is the official state bird.) More than three thousand trumpeter swans live in Minnesota. Also sighted frequently are mergansers, wood ducks, and migrating songbirds such as purple martins and wood thrush. Rarer species include peregrine falcons.

The Minnesota Department of Natural Resources lists the state's plant and animal species and maps out where they are located on its Web site (see For More Information, page 42).

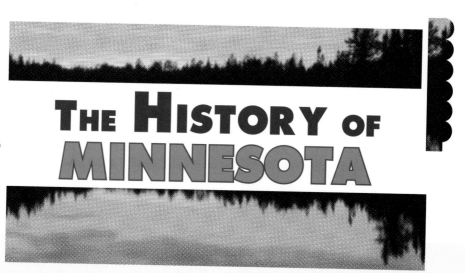

Chapter 2

THE HISTORY OF MINNESOTA

Paleo-Indians entered the Great Lakes area as the ice retreated about ten thousand years ago. They lived by hunting elk, bear, moose, caribou, deer, buffalo, and larger animals like mammoths, which are now extinct. They also fished in the lakes and streams, and they ate wild rice and other woodland foods. In time, they began to plant and harvest corn and other crops.

When European trappers, traders, and settlers began to arrive in the 1600s, the eastern Dakota people (called Sioux by the early Europeans) were the main inhabitants of what is now Minnesota. The Ojibwa (or Chippewa) people lived to the north. The Dakota and Ojibwa constantly fought each other. They had different lifestyles. The Dakota of the plains lived in tepees made from bark or dried buffalo hides sewn across a framework of poles. The Ojibwa lived in similar round dwellings, using bark and other forest material to cover the poles. They made canoes with birch bark.

Arrival of the Europeans

French trappers and missionaries were the first Europeans to arrive. During the late 1600s, René-Robert Cavelier, Sieur de La Salle, explored the Great Lakes and the wilderness in what is now Illinois.

Like many adventurous Europeans of his day, he hoped to find a waterway through North America connecting the Atlantic and Pacific oceans.

In 1678, La Salle sent Father Louis Hennepin and two other members of an expedition to look for the headwaters of the Mississippi River. Hennepin, who spent many months as a captive of the Dakota, reached a section of powerful falls on the Mississippi near the site of present-day Minneapolis. During the 1800s, as European settlers farmed and cut timber, this section of the river was used to power lumber and grain mills. The Twin Cities flourished and grew.

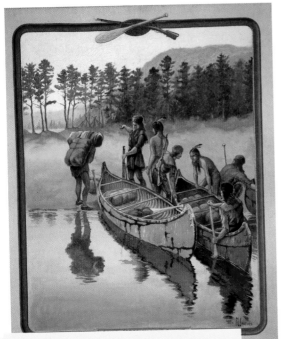

Duluth, Minnesota, is named after French explorer Daniel Greysolon, Sieur Dulhut, who investigated the Great Lakes in 1679.

Another notable French explorer of the region was Daniel Greysolon, Sieur Dulhut. Like La Salle, he was searching for a water route to the Pacific. The port of Duluth is named after him.

Europeans Fight for the Land

During the 1700s, French and British forces fought for control of the Great Lakes region. The Ojibwa and other Native Americans sided with the French. However, the British prevailed in the long French and

This print shows Fort Snelling as it looked in 1855. The Mississippi River outpost grew to become a major commercial and transportation center.

Indian War, which ended in 1763. Twenty years later, after the American Revolution, Great Britain had to give up the land to the young United States.

Farming settlers, traders, and loggers from other European countries came to the area in growing numbers. Fort Snelling, established on the Mississippi River near present-day Minneapolis in the 1820s, became a major center of the upper frontier. During the next thirty years, white settlers spread across the area. Clashes with Native Americans resulted. The Dakota, pressured by the growing number of Europeans and by conflicts with the Ojibwa, were pushed southwestward into the U.S. Dakota Territory and northward into Canada.

Shipped from Minnesota

Duluth is Minnesota's "Atlantic seaport." It ships grain, iron ore, lumber, and other Minnesota products to international destinations. How can that be, since it is so far from any body of salt water? The answer lies in a series of canals and locks that were built far to the east.

Early European explorers found that the five Great Lakes are connected—almost. The easternmost lake, Ontario, is the source of the lengthy St. Lawrence River, which widens and flows into the Atlantic Ocean. But there were obstacles in traveling from the Atlantic Ocean into central North America. There were land masses and impassable rivers between some of the lakes and, along the upper St. Lawrence, stretches of rocky rapids and waterfalls. During the 1800s, the Canadian government opened the St. Lawrence River to commercial shipping as far as Lake Ontario. Still, parts of the river were too shallow and narrow to support large oceangoing vessels.

In 1954, the Canadian and U.S. governments began work on the St. Lawrence Seaway. Completed five years later, it opened the upper sections of the river to large ships. Meanwhile, canals and lock systems had been built to connect the five lakes. (Locks are necessary because the lake surfaces lie at different levels.) In effect, this made Duluth, Minnesota, an "Atlantic seaport."

Before the opening of the seaway, Minnesota's mines, mills, factories, and industries relied mainly on railroads and trucking lines to transport their products to faraway markets. The Mississippi River has always been important, especially for shipping out grain and wood products.

Giant cargo ships cannot make the seaway passage, but most of today's oceangoing vessels can. The only problem with this "sea lane"—a combination of natural waters and human construction—is the Great Lakes climate. Much of the lakes and the St. Lawrence River are iced over in the winter.

Eventually, most of the Native Americans were either driven away or confined to reservations.

Statehood

Minnesota became the thirty-second state of the Union on May 11, 1858. By that time, an estimated 150,000 people of European descent lived there.

Many of the Europeans who arrived in the area during the 1800s were from Scandinavia and Germany. They farmed, cut and sold timber, and built flour and lumber mills along the rivers and streams. Ore mining became an important industry after large iron deposits were found in northeastern Minnesota. By the turn of the century, approximately one hundred iron mines were in operation.

A World-Class State

Its Great Lakes connections and the St. Lawrence Seaway have enhanced Minnesota's worldwide commercial links. Long before that happened, the state earned its place of importance in the Union. Throughout the twentieth century, Minnesota made increasing contributions to the nation with new and expanding businesses. It has also been the home state of notable government leaders and cultural pioneers for the past century and a half.

The Twin Cities became prominent as a milling center on the upper Mississippi River. Duluth, originally a regional shipping port, is now recognized by transporters around the world. From throughout the state have come vital materials and products—and individuals who have been an influence on all walks of American life.

The Great Northern Railway extended from eastern Minnesota to Seattle, Washington. The Great Northern and other lines made Minnesota a prominent hub of American train transportation.

Some Minnesotans refer to their state as the "Land of 10,000 Lakes." Its original nickname, the "Gopher State," came from a newspaper cartoon in 1859. Ambitious businessmen at the time proposed building a railroad in the new state. The cartoonist jokingly portrayed them as finely dressed gophers (the gopher is a common rodent in Minnesota), towing a train behind them.

Regardless of the joke, railroads were constructed. The Great Northern Railway eventually extended across the Northwest to Seattle from Thompson Junction in eastern Minnesota. It became one of the most famous lines in North America. Railroads helped give Minnesota its crucial place in the continuing development of the nation.

Chapter 3

THE GOVERNMENT OF
MINNESOTA

The state constitution was drafted in 1857, the year before Minnesota became a state. An almost equal number of Republicans and Democrats were elected to draft the document, and they clashed bitterly over the wording.

Political division and debate is as lively as ever in Minnesota. The two major parties, Republican and Democratic-Farmer-Labor, share almost even control in the Minnesota Senate and House of Representatives. Members of the weaker Independence Party hold few elected offices, but their candidate for governor, Jesse Ventura, was elected in 1998 and served one term.

Three Branches of State Government

Like other states, Minnesota's government is divided into three branches: executive, legislative, and judicial. The top-level government offices are in St. Paul, the state capital. The large, grand capitol building took nine years to build and was completed in 1905.

The governor heads the executive branch. Other executive officers are the lieutenant governor, secretary of state, treasurer, auditor, and state attorney general. Each of these executive officials is elected to a four-year term.

The impressive State Capitol, designed by Cass Gilbert, was constructed in St. Paul from 1896 to 1905. The Minnesota Senate and House of Representatives assemble inside.

Executive leaders are responsible for conducting the business of the state and seeing that laws and policies are carried out. Within the executive branch are various departments, including education, agriculture, health, transportation, housing, and labor. Most department heads are appointed by the governor.

The legislative branch of government is responsible for making and changing state laws. There are two legislative chambers: the Minnesota Senate and the Minnesota House of Representatives. The number of senators and representatives is determined by population. Minnesota has 67 state senators and 134 representatives. Senators serve four-year terms, and representatives serve two-year terms.

To ensure that laws are enforced, Minnesota's judicial branch decides legal matters. Most cases are handled in municipal courts, district courts, and special courts like tax, family, and traffic courts. A court of appeals is available to review certain lower-court decisions. The highest state court is the Minnesota Supreme Court, consisting of seven elected judges. If a participant in a legal dispute is unhappy with the ruling of the court of appeals, the matter may be appealed to the Minnesota Supreme Court. Supreme court justices decide whether to give the case a final review.

Law enforcement officers are hired by state, county, and municipal governments.

County and City Governments

Minnesota has 87 counties and some 1,800 municipalities. Each county and city or town has a government system to carry out local policies and enforce local laws.

Counties are led by elected boards of commissioners. Counties also have a sheriff, treasurer, auditor, and attorney. The sheriff is responsible for countywide law enforcement. The treasurer and auditor oversee the county's finances, and the attorney handles legal matters that involve county government.

The Minnesota State Capitol's interior rotunda includes an image of the North Star that is set in marble in the floor.

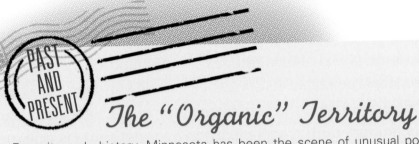

The "Organic" Territory

From its early history, Minnesota has been the scene of unusual politics and government events. Before it became a state, it was a U.S. territory. Congress made Minnesota a territory by passing the Organic Act of 1849.

At the time, the part of Minnesota west of the Mississippi River had no government at all. Its Native American population was estimated to be approximately 25,000, while European settlers numbered about 4,500. The area's leading white merchants, traders, timber company officials, and other prominent residents held an unofficial convention in 1848 in Stillwater. (Today, the city of Stillwater calls itself the "Birthplace of Minnesota.") They elected trading company official Henry Sibley to represent their area in Congress. Some congressmen in Washington questioned Sibley's right to serve because what is now western Minnesota was completely outside the United States at the time. However, they let him introduce the Organic Act, which Congress passed.

Minnesota Territory then had a governor (appointed by the president), an elected legislature, and a court system. It was also given an official seat in Congress. (Sibley was duly elected.) The new territory extended far to the west, to the Missouri River. It included much of what is now North Dakota and South Dakota. When the area became a state in 1858, it was substantially reshaped.

In Minnesota's nine years as a U.S. territory, its government took actions that had a lasting impact on the future state's history. For one thing, it established St. Paul as the capital, first of the territory and later of the state. During the 1850s, territorial leaders arranged treaties in which the Native Americans "sold" most of their land to the United States. Many Native Americans claimed they had been cheated. The white population increased to an estimated 150,000 by 1857.

Territorial congressman Henry M. Rice replaced Sibley in Washington. He obtained federal money to support railroad construction. Its rail system is still important to Minnesota today.

Cities and towns are led by elected mayors and councils. Most have their own police and fire departments, legal counsel, and financial officials.

Counties and cities are responsible for managing many types of local affairs, including emergency response (crime, fire, and ambulance), traffic control, and education.

Notable Leaders

Like other states, Minnesota voters elect two members to serve in the Senate in Washington, D.C. Based on its population, it is entitled to elect eight members to the House of Representatives. At the state and national levels, Minnesotans have contributed greatly to government.

Two twentieth-century vice presidents of the United States were Minnesotans: Hubert Humphrey (1965–1969) and Walter Mondale (1977–1981). Both men also served in the U.S. Senate.

Prominent in the judicial branch of federal government were Warren E. Burger of St. Paul and William O. Douglas of Maine, Minnesota. Burger was chief justice of the U.S. Supreme Court (1969–1986); Douglas was an associate justice (1939–1975). Harry Blackmun, an Illinois native who grew up in St. Paul, was an associate justice of the U.S. Supreme Court (1970–1994).

Chapter 4

THE ECONOMY OF MINNESOTA

Sprawling prairie farmlands, iron mines, vast forests, wide-ranging services, factories, national and international enterprises, and shipping all contribute to Minnesota's varied economy. From airplanes to all-terrain vehicles (ATVs), banking to butter, Minnesota is a thriving place of business.

Fields and Forests

Early European settlers were attracted to the territory's rich, open farmland. Farms and mills have been central to the area's economy for two centuries. Today, the state's main agricultural assets include cattle and dairy products, corn, soybeans, wheat, swine, and turkeys. The Minnesota State Fair, which has the largest daily attendance of any state fair, is held annually in St. Paul to showcase the state's agriculture, industry, and art.

One of Minnesota's most famous corporations is General Mills. It markets a number of well-known food brands: Gold Medal, Pillsbury, and Betty Crocker flour and pastry items; Wheaties, Cheerios, Kix, Cinnamon Toast Crunch, and Bugles cereals and snacks; Green Giant canned vegetables; and Hamburger Helper and Old El Paso dinner items. Cadwallader Washburn's first flour mill, built on the

Mississippi River at Minneapolis in 1866, was dubbed "Washburn's Folly" because it was so large. Over time, however, it flourished. Charles Pillsbury took over a rival mill on the opposite riverbank in 1869. In 1928, Washburn's original mill merged with others and became General Mills—the worlds' largest flour milling operation. General Mills acquired Pillsbury in 2001.

The Hormel Foods Corporation, founded in 1891 and based in Austin, Minnesota, sells a wide range of pantry and refrigerated products. Over the years, its most famous food has been SPAM luncheon meat, introduced in 1937. Fast and easy to prepare and serve on a sandwich or as dinner base, it remains so pop-

Dairy products are important to Minnesota's economy. This teenager poses with a prize-winning cow at the state fair.

ular that a SPAM museum was opened in 2001 in Austin.

Land O'Lakes, Inc., headquartered in St. Paul, was founded in 1921 as a cooperative of butter sellers. It helped establish government grading regulations and improve the quality of butter distributed to consumers. Today, Land O'Lakes sells butter, margarine, cheese, cream, and poultry products.

The Schwan Food Company, a large, private organization based in Marshall, is best known for its frozen food brands such as Tony's and Red Baron pizzas and Mrs. Smith's pies and cobblers. Pepsi-Americas, headquartered in Minneapolis, is the world's second-largest

Minnesota Timber

Timber cutting literally "built the frontier" as America expanded westward. The first European settlers in the Minnesota region cut trees to construct log cabins and to clear open space for crop fields. Logging companies hired lumberjacks to cut towering pines near rivers and float logs downstream to lumber mills. Horse and mule teams dragged logs from farther inland to mill sites.

With the introduction of steam power in the 1800s, sawmills no longer had to rely on river currents to drive the saws. Mills were built throughout Minnesota's vast forests.

Trees were gigantic—some 200 feet (61 m) tall and 6 feet (1.8 m) across at the base. As much as 2,000 board feet (4.7 cubic meters) of lumber came from one tree. That was enough wood to build a farmhouse, barn, or church. By 1900, nearly thirty thousand lumberjacks were at work in the area.

The result was the clear-cutting of most of the state's pine forests. A particular problem was that the loggers left treetops and limbs to lie on the bare forest ground. This became dry debris that was easily flammable, especially by cinders spewed by passing steam locomotives. The situation led to disaster. During a hot summer and drought in 1894, the people of Hinckley were surrounded by a horrific forest fire that was estimated at 1,600 degrees Fahrenheit (871 degrees Celsius). More than 418 people perished.

Logging continues to be an important industry in Minnesota. Happily, much of the clear-cut land, by reforestation and natural growth, is green once again.

Huge white oak logs are uncovered after being trucked to a mill in Caledonia, Minnesota.

anchor bottler (major bottler) of Pepsi products, marketing more than two hundred beverage labels.

SUPERVALU, INC. is a Minneapolis-based grocery distributor. It began as a warehousing enterprise that trucked food products to independent retail stores throughout Minnesota. It has become one of the country's largest food wholesalers.

Minnesota's forests have been key to the state's economy through-out the years. The U.S. Forest Service reported that Minnesota now has twenty million more trees that are larger than 19 inches (48 centi-meters) in diameter than it had fifty years ago. Minnesota is a major producer of forestry products, including pulpwood, lumber, and paper, which earn more than $8 billion per year.

A State of Iron (and Other Raw Minerals)

Minnesota became the nation's leading iron ore producer after 1865, when large deposits were discovered in the Mesabi Range in the northeastern corner of the state. Scores of open-pit mines brought out tons of raw iron ore. It was transported overland and downriver to Duluth. Ore ships carried it from there to blast furnaces around the Great Lakes and farther away. Minnesota remains the United States' leading iron ore producer.

Minnesota is noted, too, for its machinery manufacturing, metal fabrication, electrical equipment production, and other industries. A major developer of raw materials into household products is 3M (Minnesota Mining and Manufacturing). 3M made the world's first cellophane tape in 1932, but that's only a small example of the inter-national corporation's contributions to society. 3M employs some eighty thousand workers in more than sixty countries, and it generates more than $25 billion in annual sales. Its products include electronic,

A research worker in 3M's adhesives department explains production processes to a student. 3M offers high school students a chance to learn about product innovation.

packaging, industrial, medical and health care, pet care, safety, home improvement, paper, and recreational items.

Varied Industries

Some Minnesota industries and businesses produce commodities that are especially useful in far northern regions. For example, Arctic Cat and Polaris Industries make snowmobiles, ATVs, and other specialty vehicles.

Minnesota is the headquarters of many major business chains, including Best Buy, Target Corporation, Northwest Airlines (a Delta subsidiary), and Cargill. Cargill, said to be the largest privately owned company in United States, produces food and pharmaceuticals, and paper and energy products, among other goods and services.

Regis Corporation in Minneapolis claims to be "the beauty industry's global leader in beauty salons, hair restoration centers and cosmetology education." It has some 13,600 hair salon franchises and related interests around the world.

Hoover Construction Company, based in Virginia, Minnesota, is involved in heavy construction (major dam, highway, and similar earth-moving projects).

White Bear Boat Works in White Bear Lake is known worldwide as a classic sailboat builder.

U.S. Bancorp, a leading U.S. banking company, is headquartered in Minneapolis. United HealthGroup, a major health care services company, is also based in Minneapolis.

Tourism

Tourism is important to Minnesota's economy. Its lakes are obviously major attractions. The Boundary Waters Canoe Area Wilderness, for example, includes more than one thousand lakes and streams with endless canoe routes and more than two thousand campsites. Numerous state and national parks preserve Minnesota's natural beauty.

Minnesota is a popular shopping destination. To counter the harsh winters, the state's leading cities have established enclosed shopping and entertainment centers. Southdale Center, the country's first enclosed shopping center, opened in Edina in 1956. The Mall of America in Bloomington is the nation's largest enclosed commercial center, at 9.5 million square feet (882,550 sq m). More than forty million people visit each year. Minneapolis's and St. Paul's downtown skyway systems provide miles of enclosed walking, shopping, and dining opportunities for year-round enjoyment.

Minnesota is famous for its cultural institutions, musical venues, and aesthetic architecture. The Minneapolis Institute of Arts has one of the finest Asian art collections in the country. The Walker Art Center, with a focus on contemporary art, is best known for the Minne-

The world-famous Guthrie Theater, situated on the west bank of the Mississippi River in Minneapolis, is a state-of-the-art cultural center.

apolis Sculpture Garden with its centerpiece *Spoonbridge and Cherry*. Minnesota has many theaters. Most renowned is the Guthrie Theater in Minneapolis, started by Tyrone Guthrie in 1963. In 2006, the Guthrie opened a state-of-the-art facility along the Mississippi River waterfront. The metro area supports two internationally recognized orchestras, the St. Paul Chamber Orchestra and the Minnesota Orchestra. The state also has a strong cultural heritage for local music groups in towns, churches, and colleges.

Many annual and ongoing events attract Minnesotans and visitors. In midwinter, the St. Paul Winter Carnival features ice sculptures by international artists; a gigantic ice castle can be explored (assuming the prevailing temperatures are cold enough to keep the structure frozen). Minneapolis counters with its Aquatennial celebration of seventy summer events in mid-July.

Some events in Minnesota are unlike those of any other state. The citizens of Hibbing honor their famous musical son Bob Dylan with

Dylan Days for one week in May, while Grand Rapids stages the Judy Garland Festival in late June. In September, people in Northfield reenact "The Defeat of Jesse James," remembering their ancestors' bloody encounter with the James-Younger Gang of outlaws in 1876.

Special Services

Minnesota is noted for its contributions to national and international health care. The Mayo Clinic, founded and based in Rochester, is one of the most famous hospitals in the world. It now has satellite hospitals in two other states. St. Jude Medical, based in St. Paul, is another internationally respected medical center. Medtronic, with headquarters in Minneapolis, offers products and therapies to treat chronic diseases.

The St. Paul Winter Carnival has ice sculptures around the city. Subfreezing temperatures keep them intact for weeks.

The state is the home of other major professional services, too. In 1872, brothers John and Horatio West started West Publishing in St. Paul. They began publishing court decisions, which attorneys and judges could refer to in arguing and deciding future cases. Westlaw, an online legal case citation service launched in 1975, is one of the world's leading legal resources today.

Chapter 5

PEOPLE FROM MINNESOTA: PAST AND PRESENT

Minnesota is one of the northernmost states, which means that it is extremely cold in the winter. But to Minnesotans, cold weather is simply a part of life. For centuries, they have proudly adapted to their climate and have even come to enjoy it.

Minnesota is a state of hardy and industrious people filled with the pioneer spirit. They are also known for their progressive ideas and creative talents. Many have made their mark throughout the United States and around the world. The following are some of the individuals who illustrate the diverse talents and dedication of Minnesotans.

Ann Bancroft (1955–) Born in Mendota Heights, Ann Bancroft is widely noted as a polar explorer (she was the first woman to cross the ice to the North and South poles), philanthropist, and educator. She founded the Ann Bancroft Foundation to help girls pursue their dreams, providing them with small grants and other resources.

Bob Dylan (1941–) Robert Zimmerman was born in Duluth in 1941. Better known as Bob Dylan, he is one of the most influential singer/songwriters in modern music.

Explorers Ann Bancroft *(left)* and Liv Arnesen pose during a trek across the Arctic. Bancroft is noted for her expeditions across the Arctic and Antarctic regions and for her educational work.

F. Scott Fitzgerald (1896–1940) A brilliant author who died young, the St. Paul native wrote *The Great Gatsby* and other famous novels of the 1920s and 1930s. He also contributed short stories that were popular in magazines of the day.

Judy Garland (1922–1969) Born in Grand Rapids, Judy Garland began performing at age two. Her best-remembered motion picture is *The Wizard of Oz.*

J. Paul Getty (1892–1976) This Minneapolis native was an oil magnate and financier. At his death, he was believed to be one of the world's wealthiest individuals. He collected art treasures and established an important art museum in California.

Daniel Greysolon, Sieur Dulhut (1639–1710) This French explorer is believed to have been the first European to visit what is now the Lake Superior port of Duluth, Minnesota. He reached the western extreme of Lake Superior—near the site of present-day Duluth—in 1679.

Bob Dylan is considered one of the most influential songwriters and performers in modern popular music.

Father Louis Hennepin (1626–1705) Father Louis Hennepin, a missionary-explorer sent into the Great Lakes region by La Salle, is believed to have been the first European to visit the Falls of St. Anthony (modern-day Minneapolis).

James J. Hill (1838–1916) The Ontario, Canada, native settled in St. Paul, became manager of the Great Northern Railway, and oversaw its extension from Minnesota westward to Seattle, Washington.

Minnesota Doctors

The earliest doctors in the region were Dakota and Ojibwa medicine men. They used herbs and other plants to effectively treat lung ailments, snakebites, poison ivy rashes, and scores of other health problems. They learned to mix herbal ingredients for the best effect.

Today, Minnesota is one of the best-known places in the world for advanced medical treatment. In large part, it's because of the Mayo Clinic in Rochester. William and Charles Mayo were born in the 1860s, sons of a doctor. Their mother was also scientifically minded. The Mayos' parents taught them about anatomy, chemistry, and botany. The boys were intrigued. Both became doctors. They joined their father at St. Mary's Hospital in Rochester.

The Mayos became especially noted as surgeons. They studied the advanced techniques of their day and insisted on a sterile environment while operating. During the late 1800s and early 1900s, their record of successful operations and patient recoveries drew doctors from far away to Rochester to watch them work. The Mayos invited some of the most promising visitors to join their hospital staff. In 1914, the brothers and their colleagues established the Mayo Clinic in Rochester. Today, patients with special medical problems go there for treatment that they can find nowhere else. Each patient is examined by many doctors, not just one. The doctors work as a team, comparing their findings about each patient's situation. Together, they determine the best treatment for the patient. The Mayo Clinic now has satellite clinics in Florida and Arizona.

The clinic is not Minnesota's only claim to medical fame. Doctors at the University of Minnesota were pioneers of heart surgery. Dr. Bill Bigelow in the mid-1900s, experimenting on animals, demonstrated that lowering a patient's body temperature slows down heart activity. This gives surgeons more time to work inside the heart without causing fatal damage. Using this principle, Dr. Walter Lillehei and Dr. John Lewis at the university conducted the world's first successful human open-heart operation in 1952.

Hubert Humphrey (1911–1978)
Although born in South Dakota, Hubert Humphrey is remembered for his political career in Minnesota. It began with his election as mayor of Minneapolis in 1945. Humphrey went on to become a U.S. senator and vice president.

Vice President Hubert Humphrey delivers a speech while campaigning in 1968.

Garrison Keillor (1942–) *A Prairie Home Companion* became one of the most popular public radio program series in the 1980s. Garrison Keillor, the host, is a modern American humorist. He was born in Anoka, Minnesota.

Sinclair Lewis (1885–1951) Born in Sauk Centre, Sinclair Lewis was best known for writing *Babbitt, Arrowsmith, Elmer Gantry*, and other books dealing with social issues of the 1920s and 1930s.

Charles Lindbergh (1902–1974) Born in Detroit, Michigan, but raised on a farm near Little Falls, Minnesota, Lindbergh studied engineering as a young man. He became the first aviator to fly nonstop across the Atlantic Ocean (May 20–21, 1927). He helped design his famous airplane, the *Spirit of St. Louis*.

Roger Maris (1934–1985) Maris, born in Hibbing, was a professional baseball batting wonder with the New York

Yankees. His 1961 home run record rivaled that of
Babe Ruth.

Charles A. Pillsbury (1842–1899) After working at an
uncle's flour mill in Minneapolis, Charles Pillsbury developed
a new method of grinding grain into flour. He used steam-
powered machinery instead of water-powered grinding
stones. His innovation caught on nationwide.

Winona Ryder (1971–) Winona Ryder, born Winona Laura
Horowitz in Olmsted County, appeared in the hit film
Beetlejuice in 1988, when she was only seventeen years old.
She has won numerous acting awards since then.

Charles M. Schulz (1922–2000) The celebrated cartoonist
was born in Minneapolis. He produced his now-famous *Peanuts*
comic strip, with his lovable character Charlie Brown, from
1950 until his death.

Richard W. Sears (1863–1914) Richard Sears was a
cofounder of Sears, Roebuck & Company. Born in Stewartville,
he started his business as a watch company in Minneapolis.

Jesse Ventura (1951–) Ventura was governor of Minnesota
from 1999 to 2003. But before that, he was a professional
wrestler (Jesse "The Body" Ventura). Born in Minneapolis in
1951, his real name is James George Janos. After his career
as a pro wrestler and wrestling commentator, he won the
1998 gubernatorial election as a Reform Party candidate. He
did not seek reelection in 2002.

Timeline

8000 BCE   The area that is now Minnesota is occupied by Paleo-Indians.

1678   Father Louis Hennepin, a French missionary, explores the headwaters of the Mississippi.

1763   As a result of the French and Indian War, Great Britain wrests the eastern section of Minnesota from French control.

1783   After the American Revolution, all territory east of the Mississippi becomes part of the new United States.

1803   The Louisiana Purchase adds what is now southern Minnesota to the United States.

1820s   Fort Snelling is established near present-day Minneapolis.

1849   Congress establishes the Minnesota Territory.

1858   Minnesota becomes the thirty-second U.S. state.

1865   Major iron deposits are discovered in the Mesabi Range.

1889   The Mayo brothers' hospital opens in Rochester.

Early 1930s   A severe drought ravages Minnesota farm operations.

1959   The opening of the St. Lawrence Seaway gives Minnesota a worldwide shipping connection.

1994   Sharon S. Belton is elected the mayor of Minneapolis, becoming the city's first African American mayor.

2006   Guthrie Theater's new stage complex, designed by Jean Nouvel, opens.

2007–2008   The interstate highway bridge over the Mississippi River at Minneapolis collapses during rush hour, costing thirteen lives. The replacement bridge becomes an engineering marvel when it opens for traffic within a year.

2008–2009   A race for a U.S. Senate seat from Minnesota is so close and controversial that recounts and court challenges drag on for months after the national election. Democratic contender and former comedian Al Franken is finally declared the winner.

State motto	L'Etoile du Nord ("The Star of the North")
State capital	St. Paul
State flower	Showy lady's slipper (*cypripedium reginae*)
State bird	Common loon
State tree	Norway (red) pine
State fruit	Honeycrisp apple
Statehood date and number	May 11, 1858; the thirty-second state
State nicknames	Gopher State, the Land of 10,000 Lakes, and the North Star State
Total area and U.S. rank	86,943 square miles (225,100 sq km); twelfth-largest state
Population	4,919,479
Highest elevation	Eagle Mountain, which is 2,301 feet (701 m) high
Lowest elevation	Lake Superior shore, which is 602 feet (184 m) above sea level

State Flag

State Seal

Major rivers	St. Louis River, Rainy River, Mississippi River
Major lakes	Lake of the Woods (on the Canadian border), Red Lake, Mille Lacs Lake, Leech Lake, Lake Winnibigoshish
Hottest temperature recorded	115°F (46°C) at Beardsley, on July 29, 1917
Coldest temperature recorded	-60°F (-51°C) at Tower, on February 2, 1996
Origin of state name	Dakotan for "cloudy water"
Chief agricultural products	Cattle, dairy products, corn, soybeans, wheat, swine, turkeys
Major industries	Machine manufacturing, food processing, health services, printing/publishing, electrical equipment, metal fabrication, timber, mining, tourism

Common loon

Showy lady's slipper

GLOSSARY

anatomy The study of the structure of human and other life-forms.

board foot A measurement of lumber—literally, a section of board that is 1 inch (2.54 cm) thick, 12 inches (30.48 cm) long, and 12 inches wide.

botany The study of plant life.

chamber A legislative or judicial body; an official assembly, such as a state senate.

chemistry The study of the composition of things both living and inorganic (such as rocks).

clear-cutting The entire removal of a stand of timber, leaving barren landscape exposed.

commerce The buying and selling of goods and services.

commodity An item that is bought and sold.

dissected till A mixture of sand, gravel, and clay that has been left by glaciers in the last ice age; it is called "dissected" because the glaciers made it look as though it had been divided and plowed.

financier An investor who is skilled in financial matters.

glacier A great, natural mass of ice that slowly moves and eventually expands or melts with changes in climate over a period of many centuries.

irrigation The watering of farmland, drawing water from nearby rivers, lakes, and other natural sources.

lock A special, enclosed section of a canal in which a passing ship can be raised or lowered to the next section's water level.

magnate Someone who has much wealth and power, especially in business or industry.

municipal Referring to a city or town project or government agency.

philanthropist A person who donates substantial sums of money for human improvement and relief causes.

pulpwood Soft wood, such as certain pine species, used primarily to make paper.

reforestation The regrowth of woodlands after the original timber has been harvested.

tepee A type of Native American dwelling made of animal hides or plant fabrications slung around a frame of wooden poles.

wholesale The sale of goods at basic prices from producers or distributors to merchants; merchants, in turn, mark up the prices and sell the goods retail to individual consumers.

Minneapolis Institute of Arts

2400 Third Avenue South

Minneapolis, MN 55404

(888) 642-2787

Web site: http://www.artsmia.org

Open since 1915, the museum collects, preserves, and exhibits art works from various international cultures.

Minnesota Department of Natural Resources

500 Lafayette Road

St. Paul, MN 55155-4040

(651) 296-6157

Web site: http://www.dnr.state.mn.us

The Minnesota Department of Natural Resources provides information about nature, recreation, destinations, and other state information.

Minnesota Historical Society

345 West Kellogg Boulevard

St. Paul, MN 55102-1906

(651) 259-3000

Web site: http://www.mnhs.org

The Minnesota Historical Society houses collections of documents and artifacts, and serves as the "chief caretaker of Minnesota's story."

Minnesota House of Representatives

100 Rev. Dr. Martin Luther King Jr. Boulevard

St. Paul, MN 55155

(641) 296-2146 or (800) 657-3550

Web site: http://www.leg.state.mn.us

Information about state laws, committee actions, and legislator contacts can be found at the state legislature Web site (see also "Minnesota Senate," below).

Minnesota Secretary of State

Retirement Systems of Minnesota Building

60 Empire Drive, Suite 100

St. Paul, MN 55103

(651) 296-2803

Web site: http://www.sos.state.mn.us/home/index.asp

The office of the secretary of state is a primary source of information about Minnesota.

Minnesota Senate

75 Rev. Dr. Martin Luther King Jr. Boulevard

St. Paul, MN 55155-1606

(651) 296-0504 or (888) 234-1112

Web site: http://www.leg.state.mn.us

Information about state laws, committee actions, and legislator contacts can be found at the state legislature Web site.

University of Minnesota Extension

240 Coffey Hall, 1420 Eckles Avenue

St. Paul, MN 55108-6068

Web site: http://www.extension.umn.edu

Go here for agricultural, environmental, family, and gardening resources.

Walker Art Center/Minneapolis Sculpture Garden

1750 Hennepin Avenue

Minneapolis, MN 55403

(612) 375-7600

Web site: http://www.walkerart.org

The Walker Art Center, founded in 1927, was the first public art gallery in the upper Midwest; creative works are displayed both indoors and outdoors.

Web Sites

Due to the changing nature of Internet links, Rosen Publishing has developed an online list of Web sites related to the subject of this book. This site is updated regularly. Please use this link to access this list:

http://www.rosenlinks.com/uspp/mnpp

Atkins, Annette. *Creating Minnesota: A History from the Inside Out*. St. Paul, MN: Minnesota Historical Society Press, 2007.

Berger, Todd R. *Insiders' Guide to the Twin Cities*. 6th ed. Guilford, CT: Insiders' Guide, 2008.

Bockenhauer, Mark H., and Stephen F. Cunha. *Our Fifty States*. Washington, DC: National Geographic, 2004.

Brewer, Tim. *Moon Minnesota*. 2nd ed. Emeryville, CA: Avon Travel Publishing, 2007.

Dolan, Sean. *Minnesota* (Rookie Read-About Geography). New York, NY: Scholastic, Inc., 2006.

Feinstein, Stephen. *Minnesota: A Myreportlinks.com Book* (States). Berkeley Heights, NJ: Enslow Publishers, 2003.

Firth, Bob. *Minneapolis and St. Paul: A Photographic Portrait*. Rockport, MA: Twin Lights Publishers, 2006.

Gedatus, Gustav Mark. *Minnesota* (Portraits of States). Milwaukee, WI: Gareth Stevens Publishing, 2006.

Heinrichs, Ann. *Minnesota* (America the Beautiful). New York, NY: Children's Press, 2009.

Kelly, John. *Streamliners to the Twin Cities Photo Archive: The 400, Twin Zephyrs, and Hiawatha Trains*. Hudson, WI: Iconografix, Inc., 2003.

Koutsky, Kathryn Strand. *Minnesota State Fair: An Illustrated History*. Minneapolis, MN: Coffee House Press, 2007.

Marling, Karal Ann. *Minnesota Hail to Thee! A Sesquicentennial History*. Afton, MN: Afton Historical Society Press, 2008.

Minnesota: The North Star State (Discover America). Chicago, IL: Encyclopedia Britannica, Inc. 2005.

Porter, A. P. *Minnesota* (Hello USA). Minneapolis, MN: Lerner Publications, 2001.

Porter, Adele. *Wild About Minnesota Birds: A Youth's Guide to the Birds of Minnesota*. Cambridge, MN: Adventure Publications, 2007.

Prosser, Richard S. *Rails to the North Star: A Minnesota Railroad Atlas*. Minneapolis, MN: University of Minnesota Press, 2008.

Roberts, Kate. *Minnesota 150: The People, Places, and Things that Shape Our State*. St. Paul, MN: Minnesota Historical Society Press, 2007.

Stein, Mark. *How the States Got Their Shapes*. New York, NY: Smithsonian Books, 2008.

Zager, Anita. *Duluth: Gem of the Freshwater Sea*. Cambridge, MN: Adventure Publications, 2004.

BIBLIOGRAPHY

Ann Bancroft Foundation. "Foundation History." Retrieved May 2009 (http://www. annbancroftfoundation.org/_root/index.php?content_id=5083).

Berger, Todd R. *Insiders' Guide to the Twin Cities*. 6th ed. Guilford, CT: Insiders' Guide, 2008.

Bockenhauer, Mark H., and Stephen F. Cunha. *Our Fifty States*. Washington, DC: National Geographic, 2004.

Brewer, Tim. *Moon Minnesota*. 2nd ed. Emeryville, CA: Avon Travel Publishing, 2007.

Brown, Daniel James. *Under a Flaming Sky: The Great Hinckley Firestorm of 1894*. Guilford, CT: Lyons Press, 2006.

Enger, Leif. "A History of Timbering in Minnesota." Minnesota Public Radio interview. Retrieved May 2009 (http://news.minnesota.publicradio.org/features/199811/ 16_engerl_history-m).

50States.com. "Famous Minnesotans." Retrieved April 10, 2009 (http://www.50states. com/bio/minn.htm).

GeneralMills.com. "General Mills Across the Years." Retrieved May 2009 (http:// www. generalmills.com/corporate/company/history_timeilne/history.html).

LandOLakes.com. "Land O'Lakes History." Retrieved May 2009 (http://www.landolakes. com/ourCompany/LandOLakesHistory.cfm).

Minnesota Forest Industries. "A Lot Goes into Caring for Minnesota's Forests." Duluth, MN: Minnesota Forest Industries, 2007.

Minnesota Legislative Manual, Student Edition, 2007–08. St. Paul, MN: Office of the Minnesota Secretary of State, 2008.

Norton, Maryanne C., and Sheldon T. Aubut. *Duluth, Minnesota* (Images of America). Chicago, IL: Arcadia Publishing, 2002.

Nova Online. "Pioneers of Heart Surgery." WGBH TV, 1997. Retrieved August 3, 2009 (http://www.pbs.org/wgbh/nova/heart/pioneers.html).

SPAM.com. "SPAM Brand History." Retrieved May 2009 (http://www.spam.com/about/ history/default.aspx).

Stein, Mark. *How the States Got Their Shapes*. New York, NY: Smithsonian Books, 2008.

U.S. Forest Service. "Boundary Waters Canoe Area Wilderness." Retrieved May 2009 (http://www.fs.fed.us/r9/forests/superior/bwcaw).

INDEX

About the Author

Daniel E. Harmon is the author of many books and articles for national and regional magazines and newspapers. His geographical and historical books include *Washington: Past and Present*, works on the exploration of America and other parts of the world, international studies, and a profile of the Hudson River.

Photo Credits

Cover (top left), p. 15 © The Granger Collection; cover (top right) © www.istockphoto.com/Michael Braun; cover (bottom) © Jeffrey Phelps/Getty Images; pp. 3, 6, 13, 19, 24, 32, 38, 39 (right), 40 (right) Wikipedia Commons; p. 7 © www.istockphoto.com/Jim Kruger; p. 9 © Dennis Hallinan/Getty Images; p. 10 © Panoramic Images/Getty Images; p. 11 © Michael Melford/Getty Images; p. 14 © Francis Lee Jacques/Minnesota Historical Society; p. 18 © SuperStock; pp. 20, 21 © www.istockphoto.com; p. 25 © Mitch Kezar/Getty Images; p. 26 © Steve Rice/ Minneapolis Star Tribune/MCT/Newscom; p. 28 © Elizabeth Flores/ Minneapolis Star Tribune/MCT/Newscom; p. 30 © AP Photos; p. 31© Ryan/Beyer/Getty Images; p. 33 © Newscom; p. 34 © Redferns/Getty Images; p. 36 © Time & Life Pictures/Getty Images; p. 39 (left) Courtesy of Robesus, Inc.; p. 40 (left) © William Albert Allard/Getty Images.

Designer: Les Kanturek; Editor: Kathy Kuhtz Campbell; Photo Researcher: Marty Levick